A VIRTUE OF RESONANCE

ZAAYN ASIF

For my parents and my friends who have always helped me
mentally and emotionally

Contents

Contents

Contents

Preface

These poems.....all these words, represent a part of me. They represent the hopeless romantic that resides in me. I never understood why i wrote poems. Maybe it was my way of expressing my emotions or maybe i was trying to create something beautiful out of pain or maybe it was both. All these experiences have taught me a lot. I hope you enjoy reading my poems as much as i loved writing them.

1. Heartfelt resonance

Please don't let me go, the night has just started and the moon has started to glow.
It's so dark here and i feel cold but i know that i have your hands to hold.
I want to take risks but i'm unable to eventhough i know that fortune only favours the bold.
I know that you won't leave me but if i disappoint you, please hold me close and don't let me go.

2. Celestial affection

There wasn't a single day when i didn't think about you.
There wasn't a single time when i didn't dream of you.
There wasn't a single moment when i didn't cry because i was
missing you.
There wasn't a single time when i didn't write about you.
And being close to you was like a dream come true because you
were special not only to me but to god and everyone else too.

3. A dreamer of other's dreams

i am a dreamer of other's dreams; i hope what they hope, i think what they think, i do what they do but one thing i couldn't dream was to live like i wanted to.

4. The haunting almost

And i looked back as she went away; for the night was falling
and i knew she couldn't stay

5. Solitude in paradise

What is this loneliness i feel ?
Is this something i could heal ?
Have i lost my zeal ?
how many emotions can i conceal ?
All this feels surreal.

6. Pristine love

I remember when we used to sit together and loved to talk about forever.
i remember how i used to stay silent and just smile because you looked more beautiful than ever.
I remember how i used to ask myself, "what did i do to deserve her ?" over and over.
If only i could tell you how i felt....but perhaps i'll say it through a letter.

7. An unloved man

Love is for the blind; for the people who can see are worldly
alone and for them love is hard to find.
Love is for the heartless; for the people with a good heart are one
of a kind.
Love is cathartic; for it makes a person glow.
Love is deadly; for it makes you do things you usually wouldn't
do.
Love is hard; for sometimes conflicts can make you think that
whether it is a nightmare or a dream come true ?
Love could be the most beautiful feeling; but i wouldn't know.

8. My Beloved

I want to love you forever; Whatever comes in between doesn't matter.

Forgive me if i ever disappointed you because i know that i did....i need your love more than you know and you're the one i'm supposed to be with.

The sun is setting and i need you by my side because without you, i feel dead inside.

The fact that i was missing you is true because even when i'm about to sleep....all i see is you.

9. Locus felix

10. A way of remembrance

*And i have made you eternal with my words, so that i would
remember you forever and feel better when it hurts*

11. Clairvoyance

Someone asked, would you like to read minds ?
And he replied "what's a bigger curse than getting to know what
people thought of you all this time ?'

12. Nothing lasts forever

The past seemed hard to forget, with all the late night talks and
the secrets that were shared and spilled like blood.
He got to know her and she got to know him but, it was not to
last before one of them was gone with the wind.
Now, the past reminded him of her over and over but then he
remembered that nothing lasts forever.

13. A severance of ties

Everyday he would wait for her below her window with a guitar in hand and when the city slept he would play it so she would know that he came.

He would play until he couldn't anymore and then throw a rose at her window; she would smell the rose and then throw it back to him since her parents would know.

He would return everyday until one day he couldn't anymore. She often wondered what happened to him and why he didn't come until one day she got to know that he died since their disparities were too hard to overcome.

Whether he died or did something inside him die was a question she never got an answer to and she couldn't forget him even when she tried to.

Perhaps it was the deluded vanity which broke the two and yet none of them had a clue.

14. The final gaze

Death was knocking at my door but before going i still took a look at you for the last time.
Not because i loved you; but because you were a part of me and more importantly, a part of my own mind.

15. An unfulfilled dream

I would have loved you for all of my days.
I would have loved you in a thousand different ways.
I would have loved you because you were always worth the chase.
I could look at you for hours without any haste because you were
my home...my comfort place.
Whenever i was not with you, life felt like a waste.
I don't know if you believe it or not, but i still wait for you
everyday.
Even if i couldn't get a chance at loving you the right way and it
seemed like we were out of time, just remember that even if you
couldn't love me for the rest of your life, i would have loved you
for the rest of mine.

16. Truncated Love

I would've gotten you flowers but they would have rotten on the way because the road that lead to you was closed on me which meant that i had to stay away

17. Weakness

She had no thoughts about him in her mind but he didn't notice
it because his love was blind.
Inside his heart he felt a crack; for he had loved someone who
would never love him back

18. The stairs

I climbed the stairs but i'm still at the same place i was and haven't reached anywhere.
I was looking for a way up the stairs because hope was at play but i found out that my destiny wasn't up there.
Eventhough i did climb the stairs, i stopped midway because the staircase didn't lead me anywhere.
I stopped complaining and went silent for i saw forlornness everywhere.

19. Intricacies of affection

Why is love so hard to find ?
Why is it so complicated yet so kind ?
Why is she always on my mind ?
For how long can a person pretend to be fine ?
I remembered her through the wind chimes.

20. Romancer

Crossed their hearts and hoped to die but still there were goodbyes.
There were no if's, buts and why's because he knew that all she could offer him were lies.

21. A false face

My thoughts are killing me.
I am being torn apart unwillingly.
I'm on my knees now and i feel like i should've thought cynically.
The mind is shattered....but i'm good apparently.

22. The city of scars

He belonged to a city of scars where the streets were empty and life felt hard.
He belonged to a city of scars where the people were heartless and he was the only one with a heart.
He belonged to a city of scars where the people were evil and relationships fell apart.
He was alone in the city of scars until he saw a girl who looked like she belonged among the stars.
He felt love at that moment and suddenly his world felt a little less dark.

23. Beautiful lies

Whenever trust dies, the heart fights and people move on so easily because the relationship was built upon beautiful lies

24. The warmth lost forever

If only i could hold your hands for the last time once again, life would flow through me and i wouldn't feel so alone now and then

25. The love they had

I did everything i would, i loved you in every way i could;
sometimes i made mistakes, but i hope i made up for them just
as you would.

26. Atonement

Love me like you once did; eventhough it was me who was selfish

27. The inevitable ending

Eventually, I'll have to stop loving you.

Eventually, I'll have to stop imagining the life i could have had with you.

Eventually, I'll have to stop thinking about you.

Eventually, you will have to forget me and i will have to forget you.

Eventually, you will have to stop missing me and i will have to stop missing you.

One day surely, i will cry because you will be gone and i will be too.

I still hope that these thoughts are just bad dreams that don't come true, but whatever happens, just remember that i always wanted it to be you.

28. A secret love

He used to catch glimpses of her until she disappeared from sight.
There were many occasions when he tried talking to her, but
seeing her made his legs shaky, and he lost his guile.
He never knew if she liked him or not, and that thought
troubled him all night.

29. Clandestineness

The mind was heavy with thoughts and with no one to talk to,
life felt dislodged.
Secrecy was maintained, but in doing so, his mental strength
drained and yet he had no complaints for he had chosen this
path of loneliness and pain.

30. No regrets

*The pair met when the clock had struck twelve and it felt like
nothing could go wrong.
Although they did admire each other, both of them knew what
they had to do next but before leaving, the boy whispered to her
that maybe they'll be together in this life, or the next.*

31. Six feet under

Being insecure can cost you everything or nothing.
I saw some dark clouds that came with the thunder and thought
to myself that only i hadn't made those mistakes, my insecurities
would be six feet under.

32. Vividly Dark

The world was an unforgiving place with no hands to hold and sit by the fireplace.

Loneliness was consuming him, and everyday his thoughts grew more and more dim.

He was unable to understand what he truly wanted from the life he had got, and he had spent his whole day in a dark room with nothing but this vivid thought.

He never understood what it was that he lacked in the first place, and in that matter, he always felt dumb; for now, he lay there in his bed, for his time on this earth had come to an end.

33. Ultimate Oblivion

*Look at the graves of the fallen, where the tombstones have
turned grey.*
*Look at how easily people have forgotten them as their names
decay.*
*Do you really think that you have time, or that you can save
yourself in some way ?*
This life is a reminder that death is inevitable everyday.
*But don't be disheartened by death's sway, for while a person
departs, their memories may always stay.*

34. A loss of words

To think deeply is like a curse; for some things can't be put into words

35. The hard truth

And one day i'll be alone once again; like leaves that have fallen from a tree in disdain

36. The Man of Tomorrow

I'm the man of tomorrow; i don't feel pain anymore.
I'm the man of tomorrow; i don't know what sorrow is, nor do i
wish to know.
I'm the man of tomorrow; i'm not someone you could adore.
I'm the man of tomorrow; you could try to hate me to the core.
I'm the man of tomorrow; give me affection and you'll receive it
twice times more.
I'm the man of tomorrow; nothing hurts me anymore.

37. Darkness that lied beneath

The night is long and the darkness is taking over.
There is no hope, for the mind is lost and the light has fallen
forever.
Eventually, darkness spreads all over until there's nothing left to
cover.
Losing my good side because the bad side is trying to take over,
and if it happens, i would just want her to know that i loved her
because she would be the last person to see me before i'm gone
forever.

38. The disregard of my heart

And me being in love with you was true, but it wasn't enough for you, and i had no choice but to forcefully stop myself from feeling like i used to.

39. Tearless Sorrows

I had lost the ability to cry, and the biggest question was that i didn't know why

40. A Hopeless Romantic

He had locked his feelings of affection towards a certain someone in the mind's attic, because he had understood that he was nothing more than a hopeless romantic

41. An Acquaintance

The bond was strong, but that time was now long gone.
Memories were there to be held, but the sparkling conversations
were now dead.
Perhaps, apologies were everything they needed, but
unfortunately arrogance succeeded.
In the end, he asked himself a question, whether the friendship
was real, or just a notion ?

42. Past Mistakes

Old memories haunting, trying to forget them is inexplicably daunting.
She was everything he wanted, but he ran away from facing the reality and everything he promised.
He broke her heart in the worst way possible and while he sat in his room, his face was blank as a paper and inexpressible.
Just like that, they became strangers in the same world with memories which sat in the corner of their minds wrapped in a curl.

43. Covetousness

He liked a girl but never could gather the courage to actually tell her how he felt about her.

He used to be lost in his own thoughts thinking about her and all the things they would do if they were together.

He finally gathered the courage to ask her out but when he went to her, he saw her with someone he had never heard about and that moment broke him from inside and out.

His heart felt heavy and there was a lack of the feeling of ecstasy and if he could feel anything at all..it would be jealousy.

44. A Memory

*One photo was all it took and all the memories came back
flashing like chapters in a book.
He remembered the first time they were together and how
comforting it felt, because now he was alone on the world's end.
Perhaps, the ending was already written but it was a time from
the past which left him grief stricken.*

45. Changing times

Those times are long gone when couples were honest with each other.
Those times are long gone when they tried so hard to make things work with each other.
Indeed, time has changed and relationships now are a meaningless play and no matter what you do, not everything is supposed to go your way.

46. Moments

Why do moments pass ?
What can one do to make love last ?
How can one wish to change if he can't let go of the past ?
Are the things that are once broken cannot be fixed again
because the moment has passed ?
Maybe all these thoughts are hurting you right now to the core
but never forget that we exist in moments and nothing more.

47. The Actuality

The morning feels good..does it ?
I saw people walking in groups, a dozen.
No one admired the sky because everyone is busy judging and
maybe I'm one of them, just guessing.
I forgot that life's a great blessing.
Then the night fell and the roads went silent all of a sudden.
I went home and lay in bed but couldn't close my eyes because
sleep is death's cousin.

48. Till the night comes

The words are leaving my mind.
I have to make sure nothing is left behind.
Is the creativity dead or have i lost my shine ?
The road is long but unfortunately i am out of time.
The mind is empty with only pain residing inside.
Is the artist dying or have i lost my insight ?
Will these words be enough for me to hide ?
The night is coming and i'm not sure if i'm ready for it.
The sympathiser is dead and the fog made it blurry so he couldn't
find anyone to hold hands with.
Living with yourself is still a win but he won't put himself to
sleep because he remembered that sleep is death's cousin.
So i'll stay awake till i can until the day is done; but only till the
night comes.

49. An Interlude

Who am I ?

Where am I ?

What am i even doing ?

I have lost the track of my own mind.

Something is wrong, but i don't seem to know it.

Maybe I'll figure it out...or maybe i won't.

Maybe I know the thing that made me sad, but the road away

from the dejection is scary because it reminds me of something i

used to have and that made my mind weary.

I'm not a happy person.

I never was.

What i am, is a lost cause.

The mind is a bottomless pit of darkness; save it before you

become heartless.

Fortunately, it was all a nightmare because when i woke up, my

mind was still there and everything felt clear.

50. Then and always

Maybe we're not friends anymore, but that doesn't mean I hope for you to fall.
Maybe we're not friends anymore, but always remember that I'll be here when you need someone's help.
Maybe we're not friends anymore, but never forget that your secrets will be locked with me till the end of my time, and that's a promise until the end clock chimes.
And maybe we're not friends anymore..and this fact shocked the both of us to the core, but never stop trusting because people lie...actions don't.

51. A Despairing Idealist

His expectations from a relationship were straight out of the blue because he forgot that he lived in a world in which expecting honesty from someone was too good to be true.
These perfect relationships are nothing more than fantasies today, and maybe you are better off alone than to be with someone who doesn't like you anyway.
But still, the truth is that one day you will find someone who will brighten up your day, and you'll ponder over the question "what did i do to deserve her ?" and you will thank god everyday.

52. An Exigency

Alone in a cold room he slept.
Distance from people he kept because he liked conversations
which had depth.
He worked hard to understand the ways and adapt.
People were intimidated so they kept a gap and sure it was
lonely, but a reputation had to be kept.

53. A Loving Memory

Loving her didn't cost a dime.
Together for an endless time, because love was like sweet divine
and he remembered how she used to call him "mine".
The past is long gone now and perhaps the relationship had a
deadline because now it was nothing more than a good memory
from another lifetime.

54. Eternity

She used to play with his hair every night until they slept under the covers hugging each other tight.
Suddenly the world didn't look so bad, which was a perception she previously had.
She had found someone she could trust without giving second thoughts to what was said, because she knew that he would trust her with everything he had.
She planned to start her life with a fresh new start and that was the day the wedding took place and he told her that he'll always be there for her until death separates them apart.

55. Hopeless Fantasy

*The insecurities we don't talk about, stuck in the head affecting
us day in, day out.
The people are watching and judging every time you go out and i
can confirm this fact without a single doubt.
How long are we supposed to kill our real selves to get the
approval of a world we shouldn't even think about ?
Well, everything is easier said than done, because everyone is
chasing that approval and the judgy eyes spare none.*

56. An Addiction

Everyone chases perfection.
Can we call it an addiction ?
Everyone's busy in the act of pretension without being able to
understand that it's an act of self infliction.
Trying to be perfect is a hopeless dream though as easy as it
seems.
Somewhere in that journey of perfection, lies a part of you that
wants to be admired by everyone in the lot, but for how long can
you pretend to be someone you're not ?

57. Reminiscence

Do you remember the times when you were truly scared ?
Because those were the times that would tell you who actually
cared.
What was the reason for your nightmares in the first place ?
Was it true dark or the fear of people rubbing failures in your
face ?
After everything, did you still care about what people had to stay
when you knew that every time the conclusion was all the same ?
Start reliving your life and stop thinking about all the
opportunities missed because as you know, tomorrow isn't
promised.

58. False Hopes

He was a forgiving man.
He was a trustful man.
His nature was of a saint.
But did being good help in anyway ?
Maybe it did, but he mostly remembered the pain.
Being hurt changes people for even the most forgiving and caring
can turn evil.
Being too good won't get you anywhere because the world's isn't
fair and only some people actually care.
Maybe it's all in his head playing in a sequence like a vivid
dream or is the situation more complex than it seems ?

59. Acceptance

*Always being alone felt like a curse because sometimes the
situation was so bad that he was at a loss of words.
There is a difference between having acquaintances and actual
relationships because the latter will be there with you day after
day when time slips away.
He knows that no matter how much it hurts..one day he'll find
someone who will tell him that he always deserved to be loved.*

60. Unrequited

I loved you when you didn't, and that made me a villain

61. Every man for himself

*Lost too much time aiding others and the years went by like
hours.
No matter how much you give and care, set some boundaries
because the world isn't fair.
I'd rather be a giver than a taker because it made me happy;
being able to help someone is a blessing.
The ugly reality made me welp because in the end, no person will
be there to help, and you'll be there alone, as the world operates
on the principle of every man for himself.*

62. A race with no end

Everybody wants a shot at the world, aiming for first place, but for once, ask yourself: is the thing you're chasing really worth the race?

Sooner or later, you'll realize you pursued the wrong thing, for there was something else more meaningful than bling.

Just like beauty, possessions lose their shine, and the ultimate truth remains: you can't cheat time.

No matter the path you choose, it's ironic in the end, we often prefer beautiful lies over the truth.

63. A long time ago

*The summer is gone and the winters are here and it has been a
long time since she left but he still can't think clear.
She was his obsession back in the past but time makes people
change and relations don't last.
Without her, his world feels weird because he misses the
conversations they had when she was there.
The relationship was too good to be true and he couldn't
understand her expectations from him and didn't know what to
do.
Perhaps, they shouldn't have met in the first place back in those
years..because the strongest of relationships end and even the
toughest are brought down to tears.*

64. The Dare

Everyone wears a mask on their real faces which is true in almost all the cases.
This is the actuality of today and if you really thought you knew someone, the reality might ruin your day.
It was not a friendship but rather an acquaintance for the latter, but at least it was the thought that mattered.
Don't bother trying to know someone for real because you might end up with the feeling of ordeal.

65. A fleeting love

He saw something in her eyes and she saw it too.
The chemistry was there even before they both had a clue.
Both were shy and didn't want to make the first move because
they were scared that what if it was a "no" ?
Eventually they did get together with each other because destiny
made it's move.
But was it really destiny that had brought them together or was
it sheer luck in there somewhere too ?
Some things are hard on the heart but he hoped that one day he
will forget her face too.

66. A silent wait

He used to stand outside her window, waiting for her to show up
one day.
Days passed, but he waited and waited, and there she was one
night, standing on her balcony while the moon shone on her
face, making her look effortlessly pretty.
It felt like he was mesmerised for ages for he couldn't move or
speak and even thinking felt complicated.

67. The Villain

For the first time in forever, you thought about yourself.
Doesn't it feel good ? Being uncaring and not giving any thought
to what others felt ?
It may all sound bad for a bit but don't you think it's okay and
about time to be a little selfish ?
Don't sacrifice your peace of mind for something that won't last
for an eternal time and sure, it's a silly whine but is yearning for
something to last honestly a true crime ?
Why should you be the one to always take the blame, when the
whole world is playing the same little game ?
Why be the hero and save the day, when you can be the villain ?

68. Only for moments

Tried to forget her but i couldn't.
Tried to replace the warmth she gave but i couldn't.
She was the blood to my veins and i tried to live without her but
i couldn't.
Even though she was mine only for moments, i'll never forget her
because even if i did try..i wouldn't.

69. I'll always find you

Her eyes were prettier than the night sky and not being attracted
towards her was something that would need a hard try.
She helped him in viewing the world from a positive view and
for that he'll always love her and maybe she will too.
They were a little far away from each other and couldn't meet
everyday too but he would always tell her that "as long as we're
in the same world, I'll always find you."

70. Amor Aeternus

You are never alone my love as long as i'm there to hold you just like you would.
You are more precious than diamonds my love and i would appreciate you every minute of the day if i could.
Only if i could tell you how much i long for you but i don't know if i should.
You'll never be unloved by me my love for you were not a chapter but my whole book.

The End.

• 71 •